HOW TO RUN A **PET BUSINESS**, SET UP A **LEMONADE STAND**, BE A **HOMEWORK HELPER**, AND OTHER WAYS TO **MAKE MONEY**

by Ingrid Roper

SCHOLASTIC INC.

New York Toronto London Auckland Sydney

Mexico City New Delhi Hong Kong Buenos Aires

The recommendations and advice included in this book are based on research and expert information. The publisher and author have made every effort to ensure that the information presented is complete and accurate. Earning money is a serious responsibility: Children should always ask for adult consent and guidance when undertaking any money-making activity suggeste in this book. Parents will know best regarding which activities are appropriate for their children an will be able to ensure their child's safety while doing them. The publisher, author, and illustrator disclaim any liability that may result from the use of the information in this book.

ISBN: 0-439-57901-5
Design: Julie Mullarkey Gnoy
Illustrations: Kelly Kennedy

12 11 10 9 8 7 6 5 4 3 2   4 5 6 7 8 9/0

Printed in the U.S.A.

First Scholastic printing, February 2004

CONTENTS

Do you wish you had more money, more of your OWN money—to do with what you want? Maybe you get an allowance. Maybe you don't. But sometimes whatever amount of money you have in your pockets, in your piggy, or in the bank, just doesn't feel like—or isn't—enough.

This **survival guide** will help you learn how to turn what you like to do—whether it's entertaining an audience, helping younger kids with homework, or hanging out with pets—into ways to earn your own money. You'll also find a lot of practical tips, including how to make change quickly if you're **running a lemonade stand**, how to keep kids entertained when you're **parent-helping**, and how to **keep an audience guessing during the magic show** you put on for birthday parties. Plus, you'll learn how to steer through tricky stuff along the way, like asking for a raise, and making sure money doesn't hurt a friendship when you work with a pal.

YOU CAN DO IT!

Along with *How to Run a Pet Business*, this month's survival gadget is: **A Cash Collector and Calendar Keeper**. The calendar section will help you keep track of your money-making projects every day of the month. The cash collector part stores your coins (from pennies to nickels to dimes to quarters), stashes your paper dollars neatly and out of the way, and lets you make change easily when you need to.

You can read this guide straight through from cover to cover or skip from section to section based on what interests you most. **Earning money of your own** all starts with thinking about what you like to do and what you're good at.

Here are some examples to get you started:

If you are...	then you can make money...
outdoorsy...	walking dogs shoveling snow or scraping ice raking leaves or pulling up weeds washing bikes, mopeds, scooters, and cars
good with little kids...	as a parent helper as a homework helper as a sports coach playing with younger brothers and sisters or other children leading games at little kids' birthday parties
an animal lover...	caring for pets like dogs, cats, rabbits, gerbils, turtles, birds, or goldfish when their owners are busy or away walking dogs washing dogs
outgoing...	selling stuff, like your old toys at a yard sale
good with food...	setting up a stand to sell lemonade or home-made cookies making cupcakes for birthday parties
a whiz on the computer...	helping others find info online

Now it's your turn! Start a list of what you like to do and see if you can think of ways you can earn money from doing what you enjoy. Don't worry if you get stuck. That's what this book is for!

PUT YOUR MONEY-MAKING SAVVY TO THE TEST

Before you read this book, see how good you already are at thinking about ways you can earn your own money. Take this quiz and find out!

1. Your neighbor breaks his leg water-skiing. With his crutches and cast, he's having a hard time walking his dog. You offer to be his dog walker twice a day for $2 a walk for the next four weeks.

    a. That's me
    b. I might do that
    c. I'd never do that

2. A Grand-Prix bike race is looping around the park near your house. A huge crowd is expected. Your friends want to go watch, but you know a money-making opportunity when you see one and decide to set up a lemonade and brownie stand just outside the race area.

    a. That's me
    b. I might do that
    c. I'd never do that

3. A heavy rain floods your basement. You think that if it happened at your house, it probably happened at your neighbors' houses, too. You call around and offer to haul out buckets of rainwater for $10.

    a. That's me
    b. I might do that
    c. I'd never do that

4. Your mom's best friend has a new baby. She's having a hard time taking care of the baby AND her little son at the same time, so you volunteer to play with her preschooler on Saturdays for $5 an hour.

    a. That's me
    b. I might do that
    c. I'd never do that

5. The little boy you've been parent-helping for loves it when you juggle for him. His birthday is coming up, and you offer to juggle and perform magic tricks at his party for $10 an hour.

    a. That's me
    b. I might do that
    c. I'd never do that

6. You hear from a neighbor that a family on your block is going on a week-long vacation. You run right over and tell them you'll water the lawn and collect their mail for $4 a day.

a. That's me
b. I might do that
c. I'd never do that

7. Your parents throw a New Year's Eve party every year at home. They need extra help to serve the food and take everyone's coat. The pay is pretty good but it means missing your own friend's party. Do you sign on for the night?

    a. That's me
    b. I might do that
    c. I'd never do that

8. At your neighbor's house, you overhear their son Tim saying that he never understands his math homework. You ace your math tests every time, and since Tim is a grade younger than you, you offer to tutor him for $5 an hour, once a week.

    a. That's me
    b. I might do that
    c. I'd never do that

9. While cleaning out your closet, you find a lot of stuff that you don't use anymore, like your old Wiffle ball set and clothes you've outgrown. You decide to have a yard sale next Saturday, and you start posting up flyers around the neighborhood.

a. That's me
b. I might do that
c. I'd never do that

10. It's Saturday afternoon, and you and your friends are headed to the park in an hour to play ball. Your neighbor calls and asks if you can watch Alex for a while while she finishes some chores around the house. You say yes—you can always play ball next weekend.

    a. That's me
    b. I might do that
    c. I'd never do that

CHECK YOUR MONEY-MAKING SAVVY

Give yourself $10 for each **a** that you circled. Give yourself $5 for every **b**. Don't give yourself a cent for any of the **c**'s!

Future Big-Bucks Maker! *($70–$100)*
Wow! You know how to make the most of money-making opportunities. Your creativity, take-charge attitude, and willingness to let people know that you can help will keep your pockets and piggy banks full.

Soon-to-Be a Great Business Person *($30–$65)*
You show promise for making money! Read on for lots of ideas for improving your money-making abilities.

Could Use a Little Work *($0–$25)*
You haven't yet learned to finance your fun, but don't worry! Read on to find out how you can turn what you enjoy doing into ways to make cash of your own.

Pet-Sitting, Dog Washing, and Other Fun Ways to Make Money from a Pet Business

If you love pets, there are *lots* of ways you can earn money by spending time with them. Some owners need help **cleaning cages** or **teaching** their **pets tricks**. You can put your knack with dogs to work as a **dog walker** or even as a **dog washer**. You can also **pet-sit** dogs, cats, rabbits, gerbils, turtles, goldfish, hamsters, and other animals when their owners are away.

HELPING OUT PET OWNERS AT HOME

Sometimes owners might need extra help caring for their pets, even when they are at home with them. Pets require love and attention every day and there are times when owners just can't keep up. You can help!

Here are some money-making tasks you can take on:

- Clean cages, litter boxes, fish bowls, and dog pens.
- Play with pets.
- Feed pets and refill water bowls.
- Help train a pet or help with commands or tricks the pet has already learned.
- Exercise pets—whether it's letting dogs chase after Frisbees in the park or backyard, or letting rabbits romp around the basement.
- Teach pets new tricks.

KNOCK KNOCK!

WHO'S THERE?

Pet Project!
You can surprise pets with treats and toys—like a ball of string for a kitten to chase. When pet-sitting, you can also bring Frisbees, throw-and-catch ropes, and stuffed toys for dogs, catnip for a cat, or a new exercise wheel for a gerbil, guinea pig, or mouse.

HIT THE TRAILS, PATHS, AND STREETS AS A DOG WALKER

All dogs need walking, but owners can't always give their pups the daily work-out they need. Sometimes owners are just too busy, or not at home. A new baby or a big project might keep an owner indoors, or maybe an owner is temporarily injured (say, with a broken foot), or is elderly. Sometimes a dog's demands might just be too much for an owner to handle alone—like when a puppy needs to get outdoors every couple of hours. If you like to be outside and active, and if you like dogs, you can make money by helping owners walk their pups.

Know Your Dogs

Set up a time to meet the owner and dog before you start your dog-walking job for the first time. Be sure to ask about the dog's likes and dislikes. Many dogs have funny quirks (just like people!). If the dog fears cars, water fountains, or the growling Doberman next door, you should know it beforehand.

Find out:

- ✔ How often the owner wants the dog walked and for how long.
- ✔ If you should take any specific routes (and what routes to avoid).
- ✔ What commands you should use.
- ✔ Whether you should offer a treat before or after the walk.

Spend some time playing with the dog and getting to know each other if you haven't met before. Take a **trial walk** with the owner. Put the dog on his leash and walk the pup around the block. This way you'll know what to expect—and the dog will remember you when you show up at the door for your first paid walk.

Dog-Speak: Basic Commands

When you're in charge of pups, it helps to know their language. When you give a command, it's important to use a firm tone of voice, but you don't need to yell. Here are some frequently used commands.

Sit: Lets a dog know you want them to sit down. Dog owners often ask dogs to sit before crossing the street, before being given a treat, and right before they tell the dog to **stay**.

Down: Orders a dog to lie down. Make sure that the dog isn't just crouching—his rump should be completely on the ground.

Stay: Tells a dog that you need her to stop and wait in one place. Usually you tell a dog to stay when she's already in the **sit** or **down** position. After you command the dog to stay, she remains still until you break the command by saying something like "okay" or "let's go." (The way an owner breaks a dog out of *stay, sit,* or *down* will vary. Be sure to ask how the owner does it.)

Heel: Tells a dog to walk right beside you on your left side, with his neck and shoulders aligned with your left leg. In *heel*, a dog shouldn't stop and sniff or even look around. This is a good command if you need to hurry home at the end of the walk, or if you're trying to speed the pup past something that might be distracting (like the neighbor's cat or a squirrel!).

Come: Gets the dog to return to you.

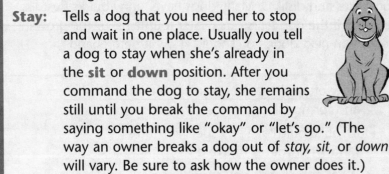

It's important to praise dogs when they do what you say. After a dog follows your command, tell the dog "good sit" or "good stay" in an excited voice, depending on what you asked the dog to do. For more info on dog training and commands, check out dog-training books in your library, or visit online sites, like the American Kennel Club at **www.akc.org.**

CREATE A SCHEDULE

Use your **calendar keeper** in your **cash collector** to keep track of when you're supposed to walk each dog. You might also want to create a notebook with info about your pooches, their owners, and any special instructions you're asked to follow (see page 12 for an example). This will make sure you stay **on time**, and are a **responsible** and **reliable** dog walker.

GO THE DISTANCE

Give the dog the same loving attention he receives from his owner. Your job is to return the pup contented. Make sure you bring a baggie or a piece of newspaper to scoop up the dog's poop. Also, be sure to fold or hang the leash up after the walk. If you're playing with the dog at home and he has an accident inside the house, be sure to clean it up and let the owner know about it.

You Can Do It!

Don't think that just because you're younger than an older kid or a grown-up dog walker you see rushing by with a tangle of leashes that you can't do the job just as well. Pet owners want the person they hire to care for their animals to **love** and **play** with them.

HOME ALONE WITH A PUP...

Once you've developed a strong friendship with a dog and a trusting relationship with the owner, the owner might ask you to walk a dog even when the owner isn't home. Maybe the owner has to go somewhere or be at work for long hours. In this case, you might be in charge of keys and letting yourself in and out of the house. You might ask a parent, an older sibling, or a friend to buddy up with you. Here's what you'll want to know:

- Are there any tricks to the keys and locks?

- Where does the owner keep extra dog food and food and water bowls?

- Where should you leave the dog after you bring him home? Should you turn on the TV or radio to keep the pup company when you leave?

Jake
Owners: Rita and Mike Nelson

121 Greenlake Drive

JAKE

- Needs to walk for at least half an hour. Likes to go down to the pond and back. Try not to let him into the water, though, unless you want to give him a bath!

- Loves to chase balls, but don't let him off the leash. If there's time, throw him a ball a couple of times in the fenced-in yard before heading inside.

- Jake gets a treat after he does his business and right before the leash comes off when he gets home. Treats are in the blue and white jar in the front hall.

- Refill food and water bowls after every walk.

- Be sure to tell him to sit at every curb before crossing the street. Praise him when he does.

- Try to stay away from kids on wheels because Jake will bark at bikes, rollerblades, tricycles, and scooters. If he *does* bark, explain to the kids that Jake's just afraid and won't hurt them. Then hurry him away.

MAKE A SPLASH WITH A DOG WASH

Often a good money-making idea meets a need when you suggest doing for a pet owner what the owner doesn't enjoy doing himself (or doesn't have time to do), such as giving a wiggly dog a bath! If you become good at dog washing, think about taking on the job on an ongoing basis. This is also a great project to share with a friend or two. You'll split the money, of course, but two (even three) people can often get this job done easier than one!

GIVE GREAT GROOMING

Make sure to soap and rinse the dog, comb any matted hair, and brush and dry the pooch thoroughly. Finish off by giving him a relaxing doggy massage by rubbing him down with towels. Whether your dog wash was done inside or out, clean up all the hair and mess after you finish drying off your pup.

DOGGY SCRUB

Careful planning and preparation will help your dog wash go smoothly. Decide where you'll bathe the dog. The best place is probably outside in a tub with a hose. Wherever you wash the dog, you'll need:

- Plenty of towels (make sure you have the okay to use them) or old rags
- Dog shampoo
- Brushes and combs

Pet Project!
Offer door-to-door pick-up and drop-off service for each dog.

KEEPING PETS HAPPY WHEN THEIR OWNERS ARE AWAY

If you're successful working with pets when their owners are home, the next step in your pet business might be to **take care of pets when their owners are away**. This is a **big responsibility**, so keep in mind you'll be spending a lot of **time** and **effort** to do a **good job**.

BRINGING PETS INTO YOUR HOME TO PET-SIT FOR THEM

Caring for a pet requires a lot of time and attention and you'll, of course, need the permission of your folks. If you can get their okay, bringing pets into your home to care for them when their owners are away can be a great way to make money. Set aside a designated area for the pets—this might be in your room, or in a basement or den. Although you're likely to need help from your family now and then—the main person caring for the pet should be you.

GOING TO THE OWNER'S HOME TO CARE FOR PETS

[I]f the owner prefers the pet to stay home, outline how many times a day you'll visit and for how long. Find out about any **house rules**, such as where the pet can and can't go in the house. Pet-sitting in the owner's home requires an extra level of commitment, especially if you'll be in charge of keys and locking up, as well as the pets. Check this out with your folks first to get their okay.

CHECK AND DOUBLE-CHECK

Before the owner leaves, create a detailed checklist of everything that needs to be done for the pet each day. You'll want specific instructions about **meals, grooming, play, sleep,** and **training.** Review the checklist with the owner so that any changes can be made. Refer to it each day as you pet-sit so you don't forget anything.

Cat-Sitting for Mr. Bojangles

Meals
Feed Mr. Bojangles
Morning/5PM

Grooming
Brush him every other day
Clean litter box every other day

Play
Snuggle, Play Hide the Mouse (his favorite game)

In case of emergency
Neighbors, George & Marley 123-1234
Veterinarian, Dr. Fuzzblatt 456-4567
Owners, Luis & Marta Gonzales
(123) 345-5678 (cell phone)

Also, get emergency contact info for the owners while they're away, as well as for the veterinarian and neighbors. And check out the pet care guide on pages 16–19 for some tips on pet needs.

Pet Care Guide

All animals need **food**, **water**, **exercise**, **love**, and a **clean place to live**. But some animals need **more play** or **more attention** than others. You'll need specific instructions from the owner on the pet's likes and needs, but you can also refer to this guide for some general pet-care tips.

To learn more, check out pet books at your library, or search for more how-tos online. You can also ask questions at local veterinary clinics, animal shelters, and pet shops. Plus, many animal rescue shelters need volunteers, which can be a good way for you to gain hands-on knowledge about different kinds of pets.

PET	NEEDS
Turtles *The turtles you're likely to sit for are of the land varieties, such as the red-eared slider, the box turtle, the Russian tortoise, the painted turtle, the leopard tortoise, the musk turtle, and the wood turtle. Water turtles are more difficult to care for, so you should avoid taking them on.* 	• Clean tank daily by changing the newspaper or rinsing the tree bark or gravel, and washing the sides and bottom of the tank. • Offer fresh water and food daily. The owner will let you know what to feed them. • Some turtles need heat-lamps to keep them warm since they're cold-blooded. If that's the case, leave the lamps on in the evening and overnight. • Some turtles get vitamin supplements daily. • Lots of turtles need a shelter for shade and as a place where they can rest in their tanks. Check to make sure the shelter isn't blocked and that the turtle can get inside it.

PET	NEEDS
Cats 	• Offer fresh food and water daily. • Scoop out messes from kitty litter daily. Change kitty litter several times a week. • Play—cats love to tangle with string and paw small toys such as mice (some even fetch). They also love toys that have catnip. • Follow owner instructions about treats and milk (despite what you might think, milk gives some cats tummy problems).
Dogs 	• Walk them and let them romp several times a day. Most dogs need outdoor time. • Provide fresh food and water daily. Some dogs have access to food and water all day long. Be sure to check with the owner. • Be good company—dogs were bred as companions, so they need more attention than most pets. • Play with them!
Guinea Pigs, Mice, Gerbils, Hamsters, and Other Rodents	• Clean cages once or twice a week, or as needed. • Offer fresh food and water daily. • Keep shelter and exercise areas clean and unobstructed. • They need a lot of exercise, usually running on the exercise wheels in their cages. • Many of these animals get more active at night, so remove cages from your own sleeping area so you can sleep!

PET	NEEDS
Rabbits 	• Some rabbits can be litter-box trained. If so, scoop messes out of litter daily, and change litter frequently. • Offer fresh food and water daily. Most rabbits eat pellets (with vitamins), timothy grass (a kind of hay just for rabbits), fresh vegetables, such as leafy greens, and small amounts of fresh fruit, such as apples, pears, and melons. Rabbits usually drink from a hanging bottle. • Wash out the food bowl and the cage floor at least once a week. • Give rabbits chew toys and blocks of wood to help wear down their teeth. • Most rabbits need snuggling. But watch bunny body language. A frantic kick, a shake of the head, or a hiss is a signal that the rabbit wants to be left alone. • If a rabbit is allowed to roam free for playtime, keep the area enclosed and remove any electrical cords. If your rabbit likes to chew, keep it away from wood or other furniture. • Some rabbits learn to walk on a leash. But before you take a bunny on a stroll, try the rabbit on the leash in a quiet place with few distractions.

PET	NEEDS
Fish *You'll probably want to stick to caring for more common varieties. Tropical and salt water fish are beautiful, but they require specific conditions and know-how. Some of the more hardy fish include goldfish, Chinese beta fighting fish, and koi.* 	• If the owner wants you to change the water, make sure you ask the owner to show you how to do it. Maintaining the right mix of old and new water for fish is tricky. • How much you feed them will vary according to the kind of fish. Chinese beta fighting fish need pellets three times a week, while goldfish and koi eat daily. Follow directions on the food package (usually flake, freeze-dried, pellets, or frozen) for amounts. But generally, offer an amount of food the fish will finish eating in three minutes to prevent overfeeding.
Birds	• Need fresh food (pellets and dry seeds) and water daily. • Water plays an important part in grooming. Some birds need to be misted with water or have fresh water for bathing every day, so ask the owner. • Clean the cage frequently. • Offer toys and exercise to keep birds healthy (some chew toys keep beaks sharp). Some birds need to climb and fly every day.

Toys, Cookies, Lemonade, and More: You Can Sell What Other People Want to Buy

You can have a great time putting together stuff that you own (or can easily make) that other folks will want to buy—that's what having a **sale** is all about. You're the seller, and as long as you have a buyer, you're in business! **Throwing a sale** in your yard, driveway, patio, garage, or in a common area of your apartment building can be a fun, money-making way to get rid of toys, clothes, and furniture you don't need anymore. Or if you like to fool around with food, you can host a **lemonade stand**, or bake and sell **brownies**, **cupcakes**, or **cookies**.

EMPTYING OUT TOY CHESTS, CLEANING CLOSETS, AND GETTING RID OF OLD FURNITUR HOW TO HAVE A TOY OR YARD SALE

One person's junk can be another person's treasure! The piles of old toys, games and other stuff collecting dust in your attic or garage might be worth something to someone else. You can clear space—and make money—by getting the old stuff out and making room for the new.

COLLECT STUFF TO SELL

Look around your room, in your closets, the basement, the garage, or storage bins. What do you have that you're no longer using that someone else might want? Consider old toys, clothes that are in good condition (no stains, rips or tears) but too small for you to wear, small furniture you no longer want, and any old sporting equipment, like tennis rackets, hockey skates, and helmets, you might have outgrown.

PERFECT!

ASK PERMISSION

Make sure it's okay with your parent to sell what you want. Whether it's your old toy chest, old board games, or an old lacrosse stick, **find out first**. You don't want to be selling something like, say, your old rocking chair, that your mom might have already promised to your aunt and uncle. The toys and games you've now outgrown—not to mention your old winter hat and coat—might be just right for your younger brothers or sisters. And who knows, it's possible that something like your old baseball cards that seem like junk to you might have a valuable collectible card in the deck that could be worth a lot in a trade—another way for you to make money (but not by giving it away at a yard sale!). Plus, that mechanical drumming monkey *you* think is annoying might just turn out to be a priceless antique. (Go figure!) Asking your folks first will help you avoid headaches, arguments, and possibly regrets, later.

SPIFF IT UP

Shine and polish your old stuff to make it look as good as possible. A little extra effort *before* the sale will help you earn more money *during* it! Patch up and spot-wash your old

stuffed animals. Repaint the rusty spots on your old bike. Tighten the wheels on a wagon. Dust off books. Buff an old toy chest. The better your stuff looks, the more other people will want to buy it!

CALLING ALL FRIENDS, SIBLINGS, AND NEIGHBORS

The more stuff you have at your sale, the more likely people are going to stop by and browse. So convince your friends, siblings, or neighbors to sell their old toys and stuff at one big sale along with your things. (Just be sure to keep whose items are whose straight by marking each person's stuff with a sticker with their initials on it, and keep everyone's money in separate **cash collectors** or envelopes.)

SELLING TIP!

If you're running the sale by yourself, you might decide to let your friends (or neighbors or siblings, depending on whose stuff is in the sale with yours) know that you'll be charging them a *commission*, a small portion of the cash they make, in exchange for having sold their stuff for them.

NAIL DOWN THE DETAILS

Choose the busiest location you can. If you're teaming up with friends and setting up your sale in someone's yard, choose the location where the most people pass by and that's most convenient for others to get to. Hold the sale on a weekend. You should start early in the morning to catch early risers and keep going until later in the afternoon (or until you sell all your stuff) so you can catch late sleepers.

SPREAD THE WORD

Write and design a **flyer** with specific details about **where**, **when**, and **what** you'll have at your sale. Post the signs around your neighborhood (on lampposts, in local stores, on community bulletin boards, or at a local ice cream shop or gym). Try to get your flyers up at least a week before your event. If you can put

hem up two weeks in advance, you might gain an even bigger
urnout. Find out whether you can place a free ad in a neighborhood
newsletter. And be sure to put up reminder signs on the day of the
event, and use arrow symbols to direct people to your sale.

FOCUS ON THE DISPLAY

Just as repairing and polishing your old stuff will make a big
difference in how much you can charge and in how much people
are going to be willing to pay for it, you should also work on how
you display everything. Ever walked into a store where all the stuff
was a disorganized mess? Sure, some people like to hunt for buried
treasure, but a lot don't! At your sale, you'll want to make sure
people stop and look around, so arrange things so that it all looks
great and so that people will know where to find stuff.

The first secret to
a great display is
**grouping things
together**. That
means you should
arrange the same
kinds of stuff side
by side. Try to
create a book nook
by borrowing old
bookshelves and
placing books
neatly on the
shelves. (Or if

you're selling the shelves, too, mark them with a price, but tell the
buyer you can't let them go until the end of the sale.) You might
even want to put a reading chair and some stools nearby to
encourage people to slow down and take a look. Put all your toys
together. Again, group similar stuff with each other, so that there's
a separate section for your cars and trucks, bikes and trikes, stuffed
animals, or games. Set up a rack for clothes and separate them into
different items and sizes. Put furniture together, and try to put stuff
like clocks and lamps on the furniture so that it looks cozy. This extra
effort will help people see how good your stuff would look in *their*
room or home.

GET SET FOR A SPEEDY CHECKOUT

You want people to be able to **pay quickly** and be on their way as soon as they want to go. This requires some extra **preparation** and **planning** on your part. Before the sale, maybe a few days or the day before, **mark each item with a price**. (For tips on setting prices for used stuff, see page 73 in the Making Cents section of this book.) If you're selling other people's stuff along with yours, you should also mark stickers with the name of the seller. (Or better yet, get color-coded stickers for each person and mark the prices for each person's stuff on them.)

Stock your **cash collector** with small bills and coins to make change. When you sell something, take off the sticker for each item and put it in an envelope or inside the cash collector so you can see what sold. If you're selling stuff for other people too, taking off the sticker with their name or in their color will also help you figure out who should be paid what at the end of the sale. (If a customer bargains for a lower price for an item, be sure to write the new price on the sticker when you put it in the envelope or inside your cash collector.)

OFFER GOOD SERVICE

Be available to greet people (be friendly!) and to answer any questions. Ever notice how in some shops you get just the right amount of help from salespeople, but in others you feel as if you're being hounded? (And in some, you can't find anyone to help you!) At your sale, you want just the **right level of service**. Circulate through the crowd and be available if anyone needs to ask a question, but don't make anyone feel like they have to make up their mind right away or feel pressured to buy something. You want people to be relaxed and to feel free to stay and browse. That means keeping an eye on things, but also giving people room and staying out of their way.

CAN I HELP YOU? DON'T YOU LOVE THAT SHIRT? IT'S A GREAT COLOR FOR YOU. HOW ABOUT THAT JACKET? IT MATCHES YOUR EYES...

THANKS, BUT I'VE GOT TO GET HOME

Haggling: How to Drive a Hard Bargain

At toy and yard sales, people often like to *haggle*, or bargain back and forth to get a better price. Keeping that in mind, you might want to set a price just a bit higher than you're willing to accept just in case this happens. However, be firm about the absolute lowest amount you'd be willing to accept. If someone offers a price that's lower than you want to accept—say so. Be confident that someone *else* will come along and want the item at your price. Sometimes knowing you're ready to stop bargaining will get someone to go up in what they're willing to pay. (And that's really the secret to driving a hard bargain—being firm about what you think something's worth and sticking to your convictions.) Of course, that might also mean that your old teddy bear comes back home with you at the end of the day, but that's what having a sale is all about. Some things will sell, some won't. Some things will be worth it to you to sell at the lowest possible price, and others won't.

RUNNING A SUCCESSFUL LEMONADE STAND

Running a lemonade stand is a tried and true money-making idea. You can make your stand a success by combining the right ingredients—**yummy lemonade** or **other treats**, a **great location**, and **super service**.

SCOUT OUT A GREAT PLACE

A busy location will definitely increase your chances of success. Try to find a place where lots of people pass by on foot or in cars. Set up your stand at a time of day when lots of people will be around. And, of course, you'll want to post signs letting everyone know where to find you.

SELLING TIP!

There's no reason your stand has to stay put—you don't have to wait for customers to come to you! You can set up your stand on a wagon and wheel your treats around town—taking what you're selling to where your customers are! Also, you don't actually have to sell lemonade. You can sell home-made orange-ade or blueberry-apple juice, or whatever else you like to make, including brownies and cookies, or your favorite cupcakes.

POST SIGNS AND PRICES

Create signs that let folks know where to find you, what you're selling, and what your prices are. Not only should you post signs on and around your stand itself, but you can also hang signs on nearby streets and corners to direct neighbors and passersby to you, as well.

YOU'RE ALMOST HERE
ONLY 45 MORE SHORT STEPS TO CASEY'S FAMOUS HOMEMADE TREATS.

KEEP YOUR STAND CLEAN AND WELL-STOCKED

Grab a table and chair for your stand. If you're hauling it some distance to a busy location, you'll want a portable chair and card table. Wash everything down thoroughly with soap and water, and dry it off before you set up your stand. You might want to cover your table with a brightly colored tablecloth. If you're serving baked goods or other food, consider wrapping up each one individually. This will help your cookies, brownies, and other goodies stay fresh and clean.

In order to run a well-stocked stand, you'll need certain stuff, like:

✔ Your **cash collector**, filled with lots of coins and small bills (a bunch of $5s and $1s, maybe even a few $10s), to help you make change.

✔ At least one pitcher of lemonade or other beverage. (If it's a really hot day, you might want to keep the lemonade in a cooler.)

✔ Paper cups and a cooler well-stocked with ice.

✔ Plenty of napkins.

✔ Plates and platters, if you're serving food.

✔ Paper towels and cleaning stuff, in case of spills.

✔ Antibacterial wipes and gel, for washing your hands without water.

✔ A trash can or bag for cups, napkins, and other garbage.

SELLING TIP!

If you're serving baked goods and other treats, cut up a few as free samples. You're almost guaranteed to sell more that way!

You want to price your goods so that they're appealing and affordable to customers. But you also want to set a fair price that's easy to work with—that is, one from which you can figure out how to make change easily (because not everyone is going to have exact change). That's why you'll often see items priced in 25-cent increments—it's just much easier to work with!

But still, even with something as easy to work with as a quarter, there are lots of possible combinations. Let's say someone hands you a dollar, and asks for a glass of lemonade (25 cents) and a brownie (also 25 cents), which comes to 50 cents total. You owe the customer 50 cents as change. Here are five different ways to give that customer the correct change, that is, 50 cents.

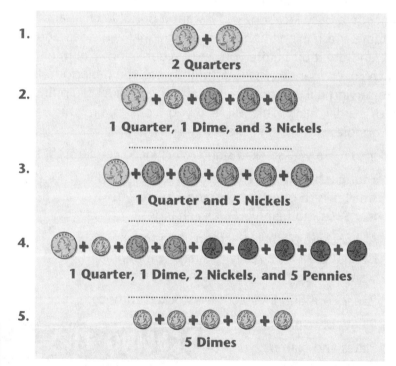

1. **2 Quarters**

2. **1 Quarter, 1 Dime, and 3 Nickels**

3. **1 Quarter and 5 Nickels**

4. **1 Quarter, 1 Dime, 2 Nickels, and 5 Pennies**

5. **5 Dimes**

Can you think of even more ways to make change for 50 cents? How about if you owed a customer 75¢? $1.00? Can you come up with five different ways to make change for each? Check the Answer Key on page 80 to see some possibilities.

HOME-MADE LEMONADE

Home-made lemonade tastes better than the stuff from a mix or a can. If you're selling home-made lemonade, you should be sure to mark that on your sign and charge a little bit more for it. With this recipe, you'll also want a grown-up's help. Wash your hands thoroughly before you start, and be sure to clean up everything in the kitchen afterwards!

You'll need:

4 lemons	cutting board	lemon squeezer or juicer (if you have one) or a fork
1 cup sugar	strainer	
6 cups water	pitcher	
knife		mixing spoon

1. Roll each lemon with the palm of your hand on the cutting board. This makes the lemons a little easier to squeeze and gets you more juice from each one.

2. Ask an adult to help you slice the lemons in half with the knife.

3. Put the strainer over the pitcher and use the squeezer, juicer, or fork to get all the juice out of the lemons and into the pitcher. Try to keep the juice flowing into the strainer so that the seeds won't land in the pitcher. If any do, you can pick them out with the fork, or strain the juice again.

4. Add the cup of sugar and stir until the crystals dissolve.

5. Slowly combine the 6 cups of water into the lemon and sugar mixture.

6. Stir everything together.

7. Chill the lemonade in the fridge for at least two hours or overnight so that it gets really cold. Store extra lemonade in a cooler or in an insulated thermos or a dispenser, if you can have one, while you're at your lemonade stand.

Once you've mastered home-made lemonade, try stirring in a cup of crushed fresh blueberries or raspberries, or a combination of both, for a fruity twist on the recipe.

Beyond Lemonade: Other Stand-Up Ideas For Selling Food Year-Round

Whether you're helping your customers warm up in the winter or cool off in the summer, there's lots of stuff you can sell at a stand in addition to—or instead of—lemonade. You can create a place that keeps people coming back at different times of the day and throughout the year.

AROUND THE CLOCK

Whatever time of day, people are bound to be hungry! Your stand can help beat their hunger and quench their thirst.

In the morning 	Sell freshly baked muffins. Serve orange juice when it's warm out, or hot chocolate when it's cold.
At lunchtime 	Make and sell sandwiches and wraps. Try a veggie one with avocado, sprouts, and cheese. Other popular ones include turkey and Swiss cheese, tuna salad, or roast beef. For dessert, sell baked goods like cookies and brownies. Pack your food in brown bags, so it's easy to carry.
In the afternoon 	Offer popcorn snacks. For an extra-special treat, branch out from the plain butter variety and try cheesy, caramel, or spicy recipes, too!

IN EVERY SEASON

What's fresh and what tastes especially good changes with the seasons. Vary what you offer at your stand according to the weather.

In the spring	Make use of the fresh fruit in farmer's markets and stores. Bake and sell mini-fruit tarts and cookies.
In the summer	On the hottest days of the year, help your customers cool off with homemade popsicles. You can start off with simple orange juice popsicles. You'll need to use popsicle molds you can find in kitchen stores. Try your cooler out first, though, to make sure that with enough ice you can keep them frozen. If you can't keep them completely cold, it's best to have your stand near your house, so you can store the pops in your freezer. You can also experiment with different recipes. For watermelon pops, mix together a cup of watermelon chunks (no seeds), a cup of lemonade, and 2 tablespoons sugar. You can also vary the watermelon recipe and substitute fresh blackberries or raspberries, too.
In the fall	Get set for the cool, crisp fall weather by making and selling **caramel apples** and fresh **apple cider**. 
In the winter	Serve hot chocolate (make sure your thermos can keep a big batch warm) with tons of marshmallows.

How to Handle Mishaps, Spills, and Other Surprises at Your Stand

An unhappy customer brings your lemonade back and says it tastes terrible. He wants a refund. No one else has complained all day and you think it tastes great.

Do	Don't
Say you're sorry he didn't like it and give him his money back.	Argue. You can't please everyone! Just remember all the other customers who liked it!

A little kid accidentally knocks your entire pitcher of lemonade over, spilling your potential earnings for the day.

Do	Do	Don't	Do
Grab your paper towels and wipes and clean up.	Accept the money, if the mom offers to pay you for the pitcher.	Make a big deal out of it or make the mom feel bad. It was an accident.	Post a sign saying you'll be right back with another batch—and go get some more lemonade. (Always make extra in advance!)

The neighbor's cat, Haywire, comes to visit. Right after you pet her, a customer comes up to your stand and asks for some lemonade.

Do	Do	Don't
Wash your hands with one of your antibacterial wipes or gel *before* serving the customer, if you can't get to soap and water.	Shoo the cat away. No one wants cat hair in their lemonade or on their cookies! (You can make it up to Haywire with a long visit later.)	Touch food or cups before you wash your hands. You want the food from your stand to be 100% clean!

Being a Parent Helper, a Study Buddy, a Sports Coach, a Computer Tutor, and an Errand Runner

If you have a way with little kids or feel comfortable with kids who are a bit younger than you, there are lots of ways to earn cash. You can work as a **parent helper**, playing with little ones while a parent is at home but busy working on something else. Or you can teach kids something you excel at—as a **homework helper**, or a **sports coach.** You can also **teach computer skills** and **run errands** for neighbors.

PARENT HELPER: WATCHING KIDS WHILE A PARENT IS HOME

Parents of young kids often appreciate having a helper around so they can get things done, like laundry, paying bills, cooking dinner, or computer work, while  *someone else* plays with their kids. As a parent helper, you can save the day and, at the same time, build experience and confidence for becoming a full-fledged kid-sitter someday, if you'd like.

If you're a boy, don't stop reading! Some boys think watching kids is just for girls. Well, that's not so! Boys that think like that are missing out on lots of money-making opportunities. And, lots of kids and parents *prefer* boy parent helpers.

What really counts here is that you're reliable, trustworthy, patient, and good with kids. A sense of humor helps, too.

Whether or not you realize it, you have a lot of skills you can bring to your parent helper jobs. You can contribute all the things you're good at and like to do, like go on scavenger hunts, make puppets from socks, or play video games.

ON THE JOB

For every parent-helping job, try to arrive a bit early so you have extra time to ask questions and can help make the child more comfortable before the parent goes off to do something else around the house. Try to get the child involved in something right away. As a surprise, you might want to bring one of your old toys or a favorite book from when you were that child's age to get things going.

GET CREATIVE: ACTIVITY IDEAS

If you plan lots of fun activities, you'll be surprised at how quickly time with your little charges flies by. Turn on your imagination and get inspired by these ideas for keeping young kids entertained!

- Read or tell stories
- Play board games
- Work on puzzles
- Finger-paint, draw, color, or create collages
- Stage a play
- Sing songs
- Make gifts and cards for birthdays or holidays
- Plant a windowsill herb garden
- Create outside sidewalk chalk art
- Create a playhouse from a cardboard box
- Dress up in costumes
- Make masks
- Make popsicles
- Write and illustrate an adventure story about your day together
- Practice a sport, like throwing a ball or Frisbee, or dribbling a basketball (though, only do this outside!)

ONE MORE TIME!

Just the Two of You

If you find a game or an activity that's a special hit with the child you're parent-helping for, make it something you often do together. That way every time you come over, the child knows what to look forward to. (And it makes your job easier, too! There's less to plan.)

IT'S HALF PAST A FRECKLE, THAT MEANS IT'S TIME TO CLEAN UP AND THEN PLAY 'I-SPY'!

Fun Games the Two of You Can Play

20 Questions

Badminton

Hide-and-Seek

Ping-Pong

Frisbee

Tic-Tac-Toe

Hangman

Hopscotch

Go Fish

Ball and Jacks

Dominoes

Pick-Up Sticks

I Want My Mommy!

Justin keeps crying for his mom, who's at home upstairs, but hard at work on a report...

Do

Try to distract him with toys, books, games, songs, and puzzles.

Do

Reassure him that his mom will be finished working soon.

If Justin won't stop crying, and is getting more and more upset...

Do

Stop by briefly to see his mom. Let him get a hug and encouragement.

Don't

Make it your mission to keep him away from his parent no matter what. Little kids are smart—Justin knows his mom's still home. He might just need to be with her for a few minutes every once in a while before he can go back to having more fun with you.

STUDY BUDDY: BE A HOMEWORK HELPER

Are you a math whiz? A great writer? A good speller? Think about what you're good at in school, and then figure out how you might share your skills with a younger student in a grade lower than yours or with a classmate. Then offer to become a **homework helper**.

HOW TO BECOME A TUTOR

Talk to a teacher in your star subject about how you'd like to become a tutor. Ask the teacher to suggest ways you might work with a younger student or with a classmate who needs help in a subject you're good at. As a homework helper, you'll want to help students to understand their homework, but not to do it for them. This might be harder than you think!

Ask your teacher if s/he can help you to find a student who needs a little homework help or coaching.

BEFORE YOU BEGIN

Work with the parent and with your tutee to understand what needs to be learned. Be as specific as possible, such as mastering multiplying by 3's or learning to write a paragraph for a book report.

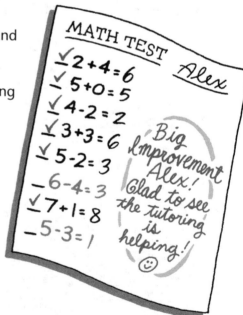

MATH TEST Alex

✓ $2 + 4 = 6$
✓ $5 + 0 = 5$
✓ $4 - 2 = 2$
✓ $3 + 3 = 6$
✓ $5 - 2 = 3$
— $6 - 4 = 3$
✓ $7 + 1 = 8$
— $5 - 3 = 1$

Big Improvement Alex! Glad to see the tutoring is helping! ☺

It's probably best to meet your tutee in a **quiet place** in their home or at the library. Wherever you work, you want to make sure the space is **free of distractions** (like the TV, radio, or bickering younger siblings) so that you two can focus. Make sure your tutee has all the necessary class stuff, such as books, pens, pencils, paper, and anything extra the tutee might need. When you think it would help, introduce **new study ideas**. For example, if Chris is stuck on multiplication, show him how to make and use flash cards. If his teacher keeps asking him to organize his thoughts better in writing, walk him through how to think about the main idea of a topic for a report.

Whatever subject you're tutoring in, share your enthusiasm. Not only will your love for the topic help you to be a better tutor, but it may also help your tutee become excited about the subject, too!

Handling Homework Challenges

Connor won't stop chattering (though he's talking about anything *but* his English homework). He just doesn't seem to be able to pay attention.

Do	Do
Keep trying to get him to concentrate.	Suggest a game in which he focuses on his homework for fifteen minutes and then gets to tell you one off-subject story. (It's good that he likes you, and the stronger your relationship, the better a tutor you'll be for him.)

SPORTS COACH

Are you athletic? Does shooting a basket, passing a soccer ball, or swinging a bat come naturally to you? Would you be good at sharing your skill with someone else? Have you ever taught your younger brother or sister to play sports? Why not try your hand at coaching younger kids and see if you can get paid for doing what you love to do and are good at? Sports coaching is another way you can earn money and spend time with kids!

LET'S TRY IT FROM THE GROUND THIS TIME

KNOW YOUR SPORT AND PRACTICE YOUR DRILLS

The process of becoming a **coach** is similar to that of becoming a homework helper. You need to figure out which sports you might want to teach. Talk to your own coach about whether you're ready now, or what you might do to get there. Ask your coach to break down *how* you teach a sport (hey, it will probably also improve your own game!). When the coach thinks you're ready, ask your coach to put you in touch with a parent of a younger kid (or the coach of a younger kids' team) to find someone who might be struggling to learn your game.

COACHING TIP
You could coach as part of being a parent helper, teaching sports skills to kids in the backyard while the parent is home.

When you start coaching, **get specific**. Do they want to learn to bat better in baseball? Are they working on dribbling a basketball? When you start, meet on a field, court, or park. (Be sure to find out if you need to reserve it first.) Then set up the same drills you do with your own team, but tailor them to the kid's skill level.

You're the Teacher!

When you coach or tutor, you might find yourself getting frustrated or annoyed if the kid takes a long time to catch on, or doesn't seem to try very hard. But keep your cool! Don't you learn new things faster when a teacher is patient with you? Be realistic about how much progress your tutee can make. Highlight and praise your tutee for what he does well. You might find that a little encouragement goes a long way (just like it does with you)!

COMPUTER WHIZ

If you're computer savvy, you can make money sharing your skill. Maybe you've always been comfortable using computers—perhaps you've even been on a keyboard since before you could read! But for some, often older people with less experience working with them, computers can be scary and intimidating. You can help! Here are some ways you can use your computer skills to make money:

- Type up reports.
- Look up information and do research on the Internet.
- Teach your tutee how to use search engines.
- Show your tutee how to use e-mail. Help your tutee send e-mail to friends.

Practice with your grandparents or an older neighbor to work out the kinks in your explanations. Then ask them to tell their friends.

THAT'S RIGHT, THE BLACK THING IS CALLED A CURSOR. YOU KNOW, MR. GRAHAM, WE MAY WANT TO ORDER A PIZZA, SOMETHING TELLS ME WE MIGHT BE HERE A WHILE...

Computer Expertise for Sale: Gift Book

Create a booklet that offers your computer skills for sale. Then sell them to others to give as gifts. So, for example, your next-door neighbor might buy your e-mailing services for her mother (who is your grandmother's age) for an hour every week. You'll help her to write, send, and respond to e-mails.

NEIGHBORHOOD ERRAND-AND-GROCERY HELPER

There are tons of great reasons to work for your **neighbors**—you won't have far to travel, your neighbors probably already know and trust you, and you know the ins and outs of the neighborhood you'll be working in. Plus, when you suffer snack attack, you're within easy strike of your own refrigerator!

UNLOADING GROCERIES

Sometimes, neighbors need a little extra assistance. Your neighbor might be elderly and unable to carry heavy packages. A new mom or dad might just not have enough hands for the baby *and* their bags. A neighbor on crutches might have to take it easy. You can help by **carrying** and **unloading** groceries. Some neighbors will need you to go to the store with them. Others may just need help unloading bags once they've returned home.

Follow these **simple steps** and success is *in the bag*.

If you go along to the store...

1. Grab big and bulky items from the shelves, and load and unload the cart.

If you meet your neighbor at their home when they return from the store....

2. Work out some kind of system for your neighbor to let you know when to run out and greet their car when they get home.

3. Tote the bags into the kitchen.

4. Put the food and other stuff away, at the direction of your neighbor.

5. Fold all grocery bags and store them neatly.

SETTING UP AN ERRAND SERVICE

For the same reasons (and more) that neighbors sometimes need help with groceries, they may need help with other errands, too. If you can walk or bike to lots of nearby stores in your neighborhood (be sure it's safe and you have your parent's permission to do so first), you can earn money assisting your neighbors with their errands.

Here are some kinds of errands you might do:

- ✔ Pick up dry cleaning.
- ✔ Pick up party stuff.
- ✔ Make trips to the nearby hardware store.
- ✔ Run to the post office for stamps, or to mail or pick up letters or packages.
- ✔ Return borrowed stuff to other neighbors.
- ✔ Take books back to the library and take out new ones.
- ✔ Pick up groceries or other stuff the neighbor already bought from local stores or markets.

When doing errands, get the cash from your neighbor to pay for items beforehand. Then keep track of all receipts, so you can return the correct change.

SPECIAL EXTRA!

Once you master errands, you might offer a speedy delivery service, as well. Then you could deliver holiday presents, flowers, cards, and other items around the neighborhood, too.

Pulling Weeds, Washing Cars, Shoveling Snow, and Other Ways to Work Outdoors in All Kinds of Weather, Any Time of Year

Whether it's winter, spring, summer, or fall, if you love to be outside, there are lots of ways you can make money. You can **pull weeds**, **rake leaves**, or **water lawns**. You can beat the heat with a **bicycle**, **scooter**, **moped**, or **car wash** ('cause you're sure to get wet!), and brave the cold by **shoveling snow** from sidewalks and driveways, or by **scraping ice** off windows and windshields.

WEEDING AND WATERING

A garden or a lawn is always changing, depending on the season, and so it needs attention year-round. Think of it almost like a pet! And because it needs lots of care, that means lots of money-making opportunities for you!

PULLING PESKY WEEDS

If you like to **get down and dirty**, pulling up weeds might be just for you. You can root out a garden's dandelions, sumac, creeping Charlie, maple and other tree seedlings, or clover. These all spread quickly.

Digging Deep

When you're weeding, you have to learn how to pull out the weed's roots and not just the portion of the weed above ground that you can see. A long-necked, two-pronged weeding tool can dig down and get at stubborn roots, even the really long, tough ones like dandelions.

At the same time that you have to be sure to get at *all* the weed, the trick is to be careful to *only get* the weed, and not to pull up any grass or other plants, too! When using the weeding tool, place the pronged head close to the bottom of the weed. When the long neck is several inches down into the ground, push the weeding tool's neck up, so that you can pull up the entire root.

KEEP AWAY!

Some plants cause **nasty rashes** and **stings**, so if you see any of these plants, **don't touch them and stay away**. Tell an adult where to find them and let the adult take care of them.

POISON
IVY

POISON
OAK

NETTLES

WATERING PLANTS, FLOWER POTS, AND LAWNS

Water is what helps plants thrive and survive. Of course, gardens and lawns need water most often during the warmer months, but depending on the climate, plants (especially those in pots indoors) need water throughout the year, too.

How much water each plant needs will depend on the kind of plant, the season, and what the weather is like where you live. Be sure to ask the garden or lawn owner you're working for to give you instructions. Just as it's important not to under-water—it's also key not to over-water, as this can make plants sick.

You can make money watering everything from the potted plants on the roof deck of a penthouse apartment to a neighbor's outdoor rose bushes to your mom's white orchid plants indoors.

SWEEPING DECKS AND RAKING LEAVES

Garden pathways, decks, and patios need upkeep. While some trees drop all their leaves in the fall, they shed some leaves throughout the year, too, as do all flowers and other plants. The wind also blows twigs and blossoms and other stuff to create a mess. So grab a broom and sweep away! Or rake up leaves. Bag everything in a special garden garbage bag.

THE FOUR SEASONS

IN WINTER

Winter is a time for gardens to rest and for gardeners to plan for the months ahead. But that doesn't mean there isn't anything to do! You can get a head start on spring flowers by planting seedlings in a sunny window. You can help a gardener order from seed catalogs. You can also attract and feed birds, and hang lights to create a sparkling winter wonderland.

WINTER PROJECTS

Birdhouses and Feeders

Not only is it fun to watch birds when they flock to a garden, birds can actually help plants grow. Volunteer to hang birdhouses and bird feeders, and to refill a bird feeder with seed. Or, to make your own bird feeders, slather pinecones with peanut butter and then roll them in birdseed.

I WONDER IF BLUE JAYS LIKE PB AND J

Peanut Butter

BIRD SEED

Create a tie with wire or with weatherproof red bows at the top of the cone and hang them all over a tree.

Hanging Lights

While many people like twinkling lights during the holiday season, some gardeners like to brighten things up with lights all winter long. Either way, during the holidays or at other times during the winter, you can help hang lights that shine in a garden all season long.

IN SPRING

You can help get a jump on the season by planting seedlings indoors. You can also prepare the ground and plant flower and vegetable gardens.

SPRING PROJECTS

Planting Flowers

Some flowers love sun while others like shade. Be sure the garden owner gives you instructions about what to plant where and how to move a plant to the ground. If you're planting seeds, follow the packet instructions. Be sure to label each plant (this is especially important for seeds) carefully. Then spread mulch around new plants and wait for the blooms!

Vegging Out

Vegetables need full sun to grow, so make sure you've got a sunny spot. Otherwise plant (and label) vegetables the same way you do flowers. In order to protect veggies from bugs, some gardeners will pair  them with flowers, which is why you might plant marigolds near tomatoes. If the garden owner doesn't know to pair them up, you might want to suggest it!

Mulching

Mulch is a protective barrier that surrounds plants, holds moisture in, and keeps weeds from growing. Spread mulch around existing or new plants.

IN SUMMER

Summer is a garden's busiest time. It needs water, weeding, planting, trimming, and lots of attention. And you can also help protect it from certain garden pests such as beetles.

SUMMER PROJECTS

Bug Off!

Offer to capture beetles and remove them from the garden. Collect them from the plants and bushes they're attacking and seal them in a jar with holes in the lid. Then set them free in a local park or field.

Calling All Ladybugs

Ladybugs offer a safe, chemical-free way to protect certain plants and flowers from garden pests. That's because they eat many of the tiny bugs that make plants sick. Get some ladybugs from your local nursery and move them into the garden. Spread them around the flowers that need the most help and let them do their thing!

HOW MUCH FERTILIZER DID YOU USE?

IN FALL

In the fall, you can help plants get ready for the winter. You can also rake leaves, plant spring bulbs, and protect sensitive plants from the cold.

FALL PROJECTS

Raking Leaves

In the fall, many trees shed all their leaves and their branches become bare. These leaves (red, orange, yellow) are fun to look at, but once they fall, it's time to sweep them up! You can help by **raking** and **bagging**.

Rake leaves into large piles and then transfer them into special garden-sized garbage bags. Don't leave piles for too long before scooping leaves into the bags. You don't want a big gust of wind to undo all your hard work!

It's a Wrap

Certain plants need extra protection to survive a hard winter. Help the gardener wrap sensitive plants (such as roses) with thick, heavy burlap. Tie the burlap firmly with twine.

It's Fall, So Get Ready for Spring?

Believe it or not, daffodils, tulips, crocus, hyacinth, and other bulbs get planted in the fall so that they'll blossom in spring. Each bulb gets planted at a different depth, so be sure to follow instructions on the bulb packs. Ask for instructions about where to plant each kind, and then mark them carefully so that the garden owner will know what to expect when the blossoms pop up next spring!

SHOVELING SNOW AND SCRAPING ICE: HELPING OUT AFTER A BIG SNOWFALL OR FREEZE

In winter, a heavy snow can stop everyone in their tracks. You can help get things moving again by taking your **shovel** door-to-door and **clearing sidewalks, driveways, and paths**. You can also offer to **scrape the ice** off a car driver's **windows** and **windshields**.

DIGGING OUT FROM UNDER

This is an ideal job for a morning person, as folks often need help **digging out** front doors and cars to get to work and school **on time**. (Though, on snow days, weekends, and holidays, you can start a bit later.) Dress warmly and protect your hands and feet with waterproof gloves and boots.

Shovel all the way down to the ground and create a pathway wide enough to walk through. Be sure to shovel steps and other potentially slippery areas. If you find ice beneath the snow, try to break it up by banging your shovel hard. Once you're finished shoveling, **spread a thin layer of sand or salt** over the walkway to prevent slips and falls.

WE THOUGHT YOU COULD USE SOME HELP SHOVELING

After a blizzard, sleet, or freeze, ice sometimes crusts over car windows and windshields so that a driver can't see. You can offer to scrape icy windshields and car windows, in addition to shoveling, or as a separate money-making idea. Get going on the ice while the driver warms up the car. Don't forget to scrape off side mirrors, as well!

LINE UP YOUR NEXT SNOW JOB

Once you've shoveled or scraped off the ice for someone once, ask if you can call them to help out whenever there's a fresh snow or freeze.

THANKS!

WASHING BIKES, TRIKES, SCOOTERS, MOPEDS...AND CARS!

You can have a great time washing bikes, trikes, scooters, mopeds, and cars. Whether alone or with friends, follow these tips to help you get those wheels sparkling and shiny like new.

HIT THE ROAD

⊛ Set up outside and make sure there's a water faucet for your hose. If you can, choose a place where lots of people pass by and can get to by bike or car.

⊛ Make sure you have:

- ✔ a hose with a spray attachment for rinsing—make sure it's long enough to reach!
- ✔ sponges, rags, buckets, soap, and a hose for washing
- ✔ soft cloths to dry and polish with
- ✔ window cleaner and paper towels for windshields
- ✔ plastic covers for leather moped, bike, and other seats that shouldn't get wet (you can use a clean garbage bag if you don't have plastic covers)

⭐ If you plan to vacuum out cars, have a vacuum cleaner on hand with attachments for narrow, hard-to-reach spots. Get an extension cord long enough to reach a power outlet.

⭐ Figure out a system for the initial hose down and the scrub, for vacuuming carpets and upholstery, for washing windows, and for polishing chrome and the hubcaps—whether for tricycles or trucks. If you're working with friends, you might want to assign each person one or more of these jobs. Either way, create a checklist so you can make sure each thing gets done.

⭐ Check over each bike, moped, or car before you finish. Then ask the owner to inspect your work to see if they want you to go over any spots again.

Performing Magic, Baking Cupcakes, and Other Ways to Entertain At and Prepare Birthday Parties for Little Kids

Do you love being in front of an audience? If so, being a party planner is a great way to make some cash! You can **direct party games** and **activities**. You can juggle balls. You can **decorate party food**. And you can help **serve**!

A TREASURE HUNT, MUSICAL CHAIRS, AND OTHER PARTY GAMES AND ACTIVITIES TO LEAD

PLANNING THE BEST BIRTHDAY EVER

You want to help make this the best birthday ever! And that means making sure the party fits the birthday child, the child's friends, and the theme. Find out what the b-day boy or girl likes and doesn't like. Then brainstorm activity ideas. For example, if the party has a spy theme, you could transform a game of "capture the flag" into "capture the secret" and have each team pretend to be a rival country's spies.

> OKAY, SO EVERYTHING IN THIS PARTY IS ABOUT OUTER SPACE, SO OUR GAMES SHOULD BE...

Once you have ideas for the games and activities, get the input of the birthday child and the parent. You should also ask when they want to serve food, open presents, and blow out the candles.

It's better to plan too many games than too few! While it's okay if you don't get to all of them during the party, you don't want to run out of things to do! After the activities are decided, make a list of all the things you'll bring from home. Then let the parent know what you'll need from them, such as prizes and awards. This way, nothing's forgotten.

On the day of the party, be sure you have everything for each game. Keep a list of all the games planned so you don't forget them!

Here are some ideas to get you started:

Hunt for Treasure

Plan a treasure hunt. Draw up a map and clues for each player. Hide the treasure ahead of time. Keep the party guests away from the hunting area, whether it's a backyard or the family room, until everyone's ready to play the game. You can get ideas from *The Treasure Hunt Book* by Klutz.

Face Painting

You might paint a dragonfly on a cheek, or a team name and mascot across a forehead. For inspiration on how to create everything from an elaborate clown to silly dog faces, see *The Face Painting Book* by Klutz or *Face Painting (Kids Can Do It)* by Patricia Silver (Kids Can Press).

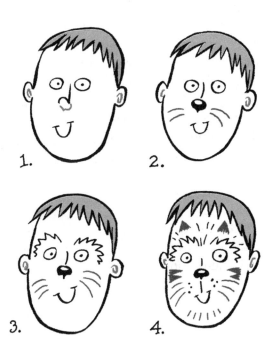

FROM MUSICAL CHAIRS TO A THREE-LEGGED RACE

Games are a favorite party activity. But it's different to lead younger kids in games than to play them yourself. When you run relay races, you probably want to win. But when you're leading younger kids in relay races, you want to make sure the **teams are evenly matched** so that everyone has a fair shot. Also, depending on the ages of the kids, plan to **adapt the rules and penalties**. Also, you want to be sure that being 'out' doesn't seem like such a bad thing by giving kids fun jobs to do while they're on the sidelines. Kids can, for example, help you pick new music for musical chairs. Find out from the parents what games and rules work well for the kids.

Before the party, **practice explaining the rules** for each game to make sure you give clear directions. Test out your instructions on a parent, younger sibling, or friend. Here are some games you can direct:

Tag

This game has many variations, but they all involve someone being "It" and chasing other people. Sometimes it's as simple as catching another person, so that they're It next. Or in games like **freeze tag,** if you're caught, you have to stand frozen like a statue (until another player who's not yet caught tags you to unfreeze you). When a player's been frozen three times, that player is It next.

Simon Says

Stand at the front of the room and have the kids stand side-by-side in a long line facing you so that they can all see you. When you say, "Simon says touch your knees," all the kids have to follow along. But, the trick

SIMON SAYS WIGGLE YOUR HIPS

is, if you say "touch your knees," but *don't* say "Simon says," the kids shouldn't follow your direction. Anyone who follows your direction without the "Simon says" is out!

Musical Chairs

Create a circle of chairs, with one less chair than you have players. When you put on music, the kids go around the circle. You should try lots of different beats and tempos to keep the kids hopping. Stop the music when the kids really get going. When the music stops, the kids have to find a seat. The one who doesn't get a chair is out. Then take away a chair and keep the game going until there's only one chair and two players left. The person who gets the last seat wins.

Pin the Tail on the Donkey

Put up a picture of a donkey without a tail and make lots of tails with tape on them so that they'll stick. Blindfold a player and spin him around two or three times. Stand him two feet from the picture, then let him try to "pin" his tail on the donkey! The player who gets closest gets a prize. You can also try variations like Pin the Nose on the Face or Pin the Propeller on the Airplane. The possibilities are endless and can fit almost any party theme.

Spotlight the Birthday Boy or Girl

Give the birthday child special helper status, such as being the one who spins the players around when you play Pin the Tail on the Donkey. Mention the child's name a lot and let them jump to the front of the line. Of course, don't leave anyone out. You should help everyone get involved and to have a good time. But it's the birthday boy or girl's day—so make it one for them to remember!

Relay Races

In a relay, teams try to get something from point A to point B before the other team or teams do. You can have plenty of kinds of relays. You can have a **feather relay** in which kids blow on a feather to keep it in the air and pass it to each other (if the feather drops you start back at the beginning). You can have a **costume relay** in which teammates have to put costumes on and take them off as they race to the finish. You can also have an **egg-and-spoon relay** in which each player has to try to balance an egg on a spoon in her mouth while walking, and then pass the egg to the next player. (You might want to hard-boil the eggs first, unless you like the excitement of using raw eggs!) Whatever kind of relay, make sure that you divide the teams equally and that you have enough stuff for each child to play.

Three-Legged Race

In this race, teams of two players run on three legs. How? They stand side by side and tie the leg that touches together with scarves or bandanas. Then they race other three-legged teams to see who reaches the finish first.

For more game ideas, check out
- *Classic Outdoor Games* by Klutz
- *52 Fun Party Activities for Kids, A Deck of Cards* by Lynn Gordon (Chronicle Books)
- *Kids' Outdoor Parties* by Penny Werner (Meadowbrook)

PUT ON A PUPPET SHOW, MAKE MAGIC, AND OTHER WAYS TO ENTERTAIN AT BIRTHDAY PARTIES

You probably look up to older kids. Well, younger kids look up to you, too! And that's why you can provide the **entertainment** for younger kids' parties.

PICK A TALENT AND CREATE THE SHOW

Decide how you'll entertain the kids. Depending on the age of the group, you'll probably need an act that's 10 to 15 minutes long. Your show should highlight a special talent, skill, or ability. You might **juggle**, **perform magic** tricks, do a **puppet** show, or **sing songs**. Whatever your act, though, involve the kids as much as possible. They can, for example, participate as volunteers, or they can shout out the answers to your questions.

Here are some entertainment ideas to get you going:

Juggle

Maybe you already know how to juggle. Maybe you don't. But this skill is sure to impress party-goers, and it's fun to learn. (See *Juggling for the Complete Klutz*, by John Cassidy and B.C. Rimbeaux.) If you decide to juggle at birthday parties, you might want to follow your demonstration with a how-to lesson for the kids. If you do, make sure you have enough balls or bean bags for everyone.

With practice, juggling is easier than you think. Throwing the balls is all about the toss and exchange—once you get the hang of it, you're juggling!

Play an Instrument

Do you play the drums, recorder, guitar, flute, piano, or ukulele? Strike up the band and play for kids during the party. To keep kids entertained, you can give them maracas, tambourines, and bells to play along. You can also combine this with a sing-along.

Sing Songs

Do you have a nice, loud singing voice? Can you stay on key? If so, show off with fun and funny songs! Choose songs kids can easily join in on.

Put on a Puppet Show

You'll need puppets, a story, and a cardboard theater. Work in ways for the audience to play along. If you're doing "The Three Little Pigs," for example, get the audience to shout out "I'll huff and puff and blow your house down," along with the wolf.

Read Stories

If you like to read aloud, share stories. You can bring books that fit in with the party's theme. Make sure you show kids the pictures!

Do Magic Tricks

Make things disappear and amaze your audience with your power to guess which card they picked from the pile. To learn some tricks, check out *The Klutz Book of Magic* by Klutz. When you perform your magic show, keep in mind these secrets of successful magicians:

1. Practice in front of a mirror first. That way you'll see your trick the way the audience will.

2. Come up with some mid-trick "chatter" so that you can talk without stopping your trick. This will also help distract the audience and keep them from guessing how the trick works.

3. Don't tell anyone why or how a trick worked. That's your secret!

4. Don't ever repeat a trick for the same audience. It can make it easy for them to figure out how you did it when they see it a second time!

MAY I HAVE A VOLUNTEER FROM THE AUDIENCE?

PRACTICE, PRACTICE, PRACTICE

Once you decide what you'll perform in your show, practice a lot. When you're ready, test your act out on an audience (try your folks or your siblings) so you can work out kinks, improve your timing, and make it work. Whatever your talent, and whomever your audience, make sure you practice, practice, practice!

CLOWN AROUND

Dress up for the party and perform your act in a fun costume. You might wear a black cape and top hat if you're doing magic tricks. Or you could clown around and invent a name and character for yourself—like the "Amazing Giggles." To create your costume, be on the lookout for old fabric,

PLEASE TELL ME YOU WORE THESE FOR HALLOWEEN

wigs, jewelry, suspenders, pajamas, scarves, gloves, suits, fancy dress stuff, and other off-beat wearable things in your attic, basement, or closets. If you come up with a stage personality for your act, try to keep it up throughout the party.

HOW TO KEEP KIDS WIGGLE-FREE

The secret to keeping a room full of squirmy kids entertained is to pay attention. What works for one party may not work for another. One group may love your juggling skills, but another group might not be able to sit still, and would rather sing songs. Prepare back-up ideas so that you can switch entertainment based on what the kids like. Whatever you come up with, be sure to find ways for *all* the kids to participate and play along.

Caitlin's Bug Party

3:00 Arrive to help Caitlin & her mom set up

3:45 Put on Mad Scientist costume

4:00 Kids get there. Pass out tentacle head bands as favors

4:15 GAME 1: Going on a bug hunt in the backyard

4:30 GAME 2: Buzzing Bees, played like musical chairs with all the kids flying around the hive (Remember: Pass out kazoos for better buzzing)

GAME 3: (If there's time) Army Ants Relay. Kids divide into armies of ants & have to beat the other team in relaying their load to the finish line

4:45 Cake, snacks & presents

5:15 Puppet show: The Catepillar Takes a Trip

5:30 Sing bug songs as parents arrive to pick up kids

MAKE AND DECORATE CUPCAKES AND OTHER FUN PARTY FOODS

If you like to help in the kitchen, you can help with the food for birthday parties. Just like the party itself, you want the party food to be fun!

STAR-AND MOON-SHAPED SANDWICHES

Use cookie cutters to cut bread into fantastic shapes like stars, moons, animals, or letters of the alphabet to spell the birthday child's name. Fill the shapes with peanut butter and jelly, cheese, or tuna fish to make sandwiches.

MAKE FUNNY FACES

Spread pizza toppings into the shape of a face with, say, pepperoni as the eyes, a mushroom as a nose, and red pepper as a mouth. You can also arrange fruits and veggies into faces, with grapes for eyes, a strawberry for a nose, and a slice of banana as a surprised "oh" expression for a mouth.

DECORATE CUPCAKES

Cupcakes can be as much fun as cake because each child gets their own! Try to match the cupcakes to the party theme, so that a train party can have different color engines, a princess party might have diamonds, and an undersea party can have schools of fish. You can use a cake mix, store-bought frostings, and candies.

Or you can try to make your cupcakes from scratch (with a grown-up's help). Whatever the design, make sure the birthday child's cupcake is extra-special, and be sure to leave room for candles!

From A to Z

Top off a frosted cupcake with candy or frosting letters, or personalize them with each party guest's name. Finish off with candy circles, dots, or confetti. You can also use frosting and candles to make animal faces, cars, monsters, or a child's favorite book characters.

BUT I'M LINDSEY!

When you use names for a party, whether on cupcakes or name tags, be sure to double-check spelling.

How To Help Make The Party Fun

At a birthday party, you can also earn money **serving food**, **decorating**, and **cleaning up**.

1. **Dress the part.** Your outfit can let people know you're there to help. You might wear a funny hat or something that goes with the theme so that kids and grown-ups can spot you in the crowd.

2. **Know what to do.** The host might want you to stay out of the way, cleaning up and helping out in the kitchen. Or you might be asked to be in the middle of the party, making sure everything runs smoothly.

3. **Set the stage.** Before the party, you can help decorate, prepare, and arrange the food, flowers, or any favors. You might also help set up any games.

4. **Once the party begins,** you might meet and greet the guests, take and put away coats and bags, put any presents on a table, and direct everyone to the action.

5. **Throughout the party,** you can help serve food and drinks, and restock and refill food platters, napkins, and beverages. You can also listen up for any lulls in the music and keep it playing.

6. **As the party finishes,** deliver coats and any backpacks or bags back to the party guests. Then stick around to **help with clean-up**.

Making Cents: How to Start and Succeed in Your Own Business

By now you're probably excited about all the fun businesses you can start! In this chapter, you'll find out how to **set the right price** and how to **let people know you're out there**. Plus, you'll get advice on **how to ask for more money** and **how to keep track of what you earn**.

GETTING A GREAT START

So, you've got the world's greatest idea to make money and you can't wait to begin. But hold on! Have you decided how you'll let people know about you? Can you do it alone, or should you ask a friend to pitch in? What should you charge? Thinking ahead will help you get your business off to a great start!

TEST IT OUT

Before you invest too much time and energy in your business, make sure you can find customers who are interested in your idea! Ask around. Is anyone interested in your errand service? Don't be discouraged if someone *else* is already doing something similar to your idea. If a busy dog walker already exercises pooches in your neighborhood, you don't need to give up if you have your heart set on walking dogs, too. Try to think about how you can beat the competition. Maybe you can offer a better price, or the same service at a different time. Perhaps that adult dog walker exercises pups mostly during the week. If you're planning on walking dogs on the weekends when you have more time anyway, you might just be in business!

CAN YOU FIND THE TIME?

Think about how much time you can spend earning money. You may love the idea (and the high pay) of being a parent helper for your neighbor two afternoons a week. But when you factor in your homework, soccer practice, piano lessons and tae kwon do, you might realize you just don't have enough extra time!

Be realistic about how much you can take on. When launching a business, it's important to do what you say you will. You're better off starting small rather than over-promising and making your customers mad when you can't deliver. And when you're counting up your time, be sure you leave enough to have fun with your friends.

Also remember that there are ways to be creative about your time. If you're too busy during the school week, think about weekend ways to make money. Or, plan to make money during summer vacations and holidays. If you're a morning person, come up with ways to earn money in the early hours of the day, and remember that you can always get some help by teaming up with a friend.

HEY! – WHEN WILL I FIT IN MY DOG WALKING SERVICE?

9:00

8am–3pm – School

3pm–5pm – Soccer

5:30pm – Dinner

6:30pm – Tae Kwon Do

7:30pm – Piano Practice

8:30pm – Homework

TEAM UP WITH A FRIEND!

Sometimes, you and a friend can **make more money** and **get more done in less time** by **working together**. As they say, two heads (and two sets of hands) are often better than one! Certain money-making ideas lend themselves particularly well to working with friends, like:

- ✪ Entertaining at birthday parties

- ✪ Washing dogs

- ✪ Parent-helping for more than one child at a time

- ✪ Holding a garage or toy sale

- ✪ Raking leaves, shoveling snow, or scraping ice

- ✪ Holding a bike, trike, moped, or car wash

- ✪ Pet-sitting in the pet owner's home (if you have to make lots of visits in a day, you can share the responsibility)

Friendship First: How to make sure making money doesn't get in the way

Follow these tips to help you work well together.

1. Share the work equally. Sure, one of you might be better at vacuuming cars while the other likes to polish windows when you have a car wash. It's okay to take on different roles, depending on what each of you likes and is good at. But divide the work fairly.

2. Talk about what's bothering you. If you get annoyed or angry about the way something was handled, talk about it. Try not to accuse or blame your friend. Try to phrase the problem in less threatening ways, such as saying, "When you went home early before the job was done, it made me feel like I do all the work."

3. Treat each other like friends. Hey! You're friends because you like each other. So treat each other that way. Don't boss your friend around. Don't bicker and argue. And be sure to tell your friend when they do a good job!

4. Keep your sense of humor. When you're working together to earn money, sometimes the best thing to do when something goes wrong is to laugh about it.

5. Know when to call it quits. If you've tried everything and you keep getting on each other's nerves, maybe you weren't meant to make money together. It's better to quit working together than to quit being friends!

A business card offers a quick way for someone to remember and contact you. It should be small and wallet-sized, approximately the same size as a library card or your smallest school photo. The most important information to include is your **name**, **what you do**, and your **phone number**. You can buy blank business cards in office or art supply stores, or cut them out of stiff paper. Fill them out by hand or print them out on the computer and hand them out to friends, neighbors, and relatives to help spread the word about your business.

When you work at a party, for example, be sure to have extra cards with you in case any of the other parents want to reach you later to hire you for *their* child's party.

Loves all kinds of celebrations, especially birthdays!
Will decorate, bake cupcakes,
set up, serve and clean up.

ANNA 555-3849

SELL YOURSELF

You'll need to let people know about your business idea. Start with your family, friends, neighbors and other people you know—in person, by phone or by e-mail. Make **flyers** and **business cards** and hand them out.

To convince people to try you out, you might offer to do the first job for free, or give a discount, like a special introductory offer of $1.00 off the first hour of parent-helping.

SETTING A PRICE THAT'S FAIR

A fair price means that it's fair for you and fair for the person you're working for or selling something to. Here are some things to keep in mind to get to a fair price.

For something you do...

Check around to see what other people charge for the same service or sale item. Then factor in your age and your experience and what you'll be doing. If you're going to need extra materials, like favors for a birthday party, make sure you and the person you're working for decide who will get and pay for it. You should make sure the person pays you back, if you get the stuff, or that these materials are included in your price.

For something you make...

Whether you print out and sell birthday cards on the computer or make great home-made cookies, you need to be sure the price for each item covers your costs and pays you a little extra, which is your *profit*. First, add up the costs of all the materials you used. Then figure out how much more you should charge to pay for your time and effort.

For something old you're selling to someone else...

When pricing your old toys, books, and stuff for a yard or toy sale, check for wear and tear. You can charge more for things in better condition than for more worn-out things.

Don't work for someone without setting a price first

Setting the price ahead of time for work you do or things you make will ensure you're paid fairly and will help put a stop to any misunderstandings or confusion before they develop.

THIS IS FOR TWO HOURS OF MATH HELP?

How to negotiate and drive a hard bargain

Sometimes when you are trying to set a price with a customer, you may have to *negotiate*, which is the back and forth process of bargaining to get a price or a rate that's fair to both of you. It's a lot like *haggling* (see page 25 for tips), so you might start off by asking for a price higher than you'd be willing to accept. For example, if you would like to rake leaves for five dollars, you might want to suggest eight first so that if the customer comes back with three, you can meet in the middle and both of you will feel as if you have won something. Be firm about what amount you need to earn and don't be afraid to say no to a job that won't pay enough to make your time and effort worthwhile.

BECOME AN EXPERT

Your customers hire you because you have special skills. Continuing to develop your know-how is an important way to keep your customers happy and win more jobs (and eventually charge more, too!). So help your dad make brownies on weekends, if you're going to want to sell baked goodies. Talk to a professional animal groomer, if you're going to hold a dog wash. Be on the lookout for ways to learn more and do a better job!

BE PROFESSIONAL

Getting someone to hire you is one thing. Getting them to hire you a second, third, fourth, or fifth time and to tell all their friends about you is another! The way to set yourself apart and be asked back again and again is by being professional. And that means being **on time**, **polite**, **thorough**, **responsible**, **friendly**, and **open to suggestions**. It also means **doing your best** every time.

JUST SAY NO: HOW TO SURVIVE BAD BOSSES, BAD DEALS, AND STAY SAFE IN ALMOST ANY BUSINESS SITUATION

You may have heard that the customer is always right, but if anyone ever makes you nervous or uncomfortable for any reason, stop working for them immediately and inform an adult. Sometimes there's a lot of pressure on kids to be polite, especially to adults. But remember that you always have the right to say no!

Always tell a parent, or other trustworthy adult, where you're working. And trust your instincts if a person makes you feel creepy.

If an adult is supposed to drive you home and they seem strange or make you feel weird in any way, call your parent or someone else to come and get you. The same goes for when someone asks you to do something that seems like a bad idea. If a customer asks you to do something you don't think is safe, such as climb a too-tall ladder, remember that you have the right to say no. And, what should you do if an adult tries to get you to work for a bargain basement price? Don't let anyone take advantage of you just because you're a kid. If it doesn't feel like a fair deal, stand up for yourself and say so!

HOW TO KEEP YOUR BUSINESS RUNNING SMOOTHLY

Once you start your business, you'll want to make sure it runs smoothly. You can do that by **keeping track of how much money you earn** and **finding ways to improve your business**. After you've been at something a while and you're getting better and better at it, you might want to **ask for a raise**. Whatever you're doing, remember it pays to **give great service**, and to let people know what else you can do.

MONEY IN YOUR POCKET

You'll need to keep track of what you're paid, what you're owed, and what you spend on materials and supplies. Here's an example.

MY HAPPY BIRTHDAY COMPANY			
DATE	FOR WHAT	WHAT I SPEND	WHAT I'M OWED
6/15	Caitlyn's Party	$2.00 Balloons	$17.00 2+15
6/12	Michael's Party	$4.00 Cupcake Stuff	$20.00 4+16

Write what you spend in one column and what you're owed in another column. In this example, you paid $2 for balloons for Caitlyn's party and are getting $15 for planning the party, so you're owed $17 total. Knowing how much money's on hand is one way to tell how your business is doing.

ASKING FOR A RAISE

Sometimes after you've been working for someone a while, you might realize you need to make more money for the time you put in. Say you've cared for your neighbor's cat, Mr. Bojangles, for over a year and you love him. But when you take a look at your schedule, you realize you need to earn more to justify all that effort and energy.

It can be nerve-racking to ask for a pay increase, so here are some ideas to make the conversation easier.

- ✔ **Make a list.** Write down all the reasons you feel you deserve a raise. If you think you'll forget what you want to say, bring the list along to remind you.

- ✔ **Set an appointment.** It's best to ask for a raise in person, but if you don't see the pet's owner regularly, you can phone or write a note, or send an e-mail.

- ✔ **Explain the situation.** Be clear about your reasons. Be specific about how much more you need to earn. You may even want to ask for a little more than you really want, in case your neighbor comes back with an offer somewhere in the middle. (This is called negotiation, when you and your customer go back and forth to set a fair price. For more tips on negotiation, see page 73.)

- ✔ **Back up your argument.** Don't be afraid to sell yourself. Also, find out what other people charge and compare your prices. If you will still be less expensive than what others charge, be sure to let the customer know.

There's always the possibility that, even after hearing your carefully prepared argument, the customer won't give you the raise. If you decide to stop working together, be friendly about it.

GIVE GREAT SERVICE

Want to know how to keep your customers happy and get them to tell their friends about you? Exceed their expectations! Ask what you can do better next time and do it! Try to do just a little bit *more* than your customers ask of you.

HOW DID YOU EVER FIND THE TIME TO ALPHABETIZE CHLOE'S CRAYONS?

Know How and When to Use a Reference

A *reference* is a person who knows you and your work. When you're meeting a potential customer about a new job, whether it's homework helping or dog walking, putting them in touch with a reference gives them a chance to hear what a great job you've done for other people. And remember, when someone acts as a reference for you, that person is doing you a favor. Be sure to say "thank you"!

SPEAK UP

Don't be shy. If you walk someone's dog, you might tell that person you also water lawns while your neighbors are on vacation. You're likely to make more money if you let people know about all your various skills. Don't worry, you aren't bragging. You're learning to spread the word and make the most of your opportunities!

PERSISTENCE PAYS

So maybe you've created the world's best birthday party show, complete with a finale in which you juggle pineapples, but you only told a couple of friends and no one ever called to hire you. Don't give up! Clearly you need to let more people know about your talents. Make a flyer and hand it out around to the neighbors on your block. Talk to family, friends, or parents whose kids you know or watch.

Okay, so now you're making money. What do you do with it after you have it? Do you spend it right away? Well, sure—some of it, anyway. But what if you want to buy something BIG and you don't yet have enough earned up? How do you save for it?

OKAY, SO IF I SAVE $10 A WEEK, AND DON'T SPEND MY BIRTHDAY MONEY, I CAN GET MY MP3 PLAYER IN 3 MONTHS! **YEAH!**

SAVING FOR SOMETHING BIG?

These simple tips can help boost your savings.

1. **Stop and wait before you buy.** Sometimes if you go home and think about it, a little distance and time will change your mind. But if you still want to buy it the next day or the next week, you'll know you won't regret it.

2. **Shop around.** Can you find a better price? Can you clip coupons or get it for less at a discount store? A little extra searching and smart shopping can save you money in the long run.

3. **Give yourself an allowance.** Make sure you give yourself enough money to have fun now *and* still save. Giving yourself a limit for how much you can spend helps. Before you head out to meet your friends, think about how much money you have, how

much you need for the next month, and how much you need to meet your goal. Then give yourself a dollar amount you can spend while you're with your friends—and don't exceed it.

4. **Think of creative ways to save.** Can you invite your friends over and rent a video instead of going out to see a movie in the theater? Can you convince your friends to take a long bike ride instead of going to the diner for lunch? Can you draw a homemade birthday card or print one out on the computer? Cutting back on some expenses will help you reach your goal.

GO FOR IT!

Whatever you dream, you can do it, whether it's starting a business of your own or saving up for something you've always wanted. It may take longer than you think, but you can do it, if it's worth it to you!

Two More Ways to Get to 50¢ (page 28)

1. 1 Quarter, 2 Dimes, and 1 Nickel
2. 1 Quarter, 4 Nickels, and 5 Pennies

Five Ways to Get to 75¢

1. 3 Quarters

2. 2 Quarters, 2 Dimes, and 1 Nickel

3. 7 Dimes and 1 Nickel

4. 1 Quarter and 5 Dimes

5. 2 Quarters and 5 Nickels

Five Ways to Get to $1.00

1. 4 Quarters

2. 3 Quarters, 2 Dimes, and 1 Nickel

3. 2 Quarters and 5 Dimes

4. 3 Quarters and 5 Nickels

5. 10 Dimes